to you, my dear book
in the midst of darkness
you lightened up my being
as I sat behind my desk
I knew I had
to bring you into light
even though I was afraid
to give you my heart and not my mind
but here you are
in front of me with all of your pages
I've written and called you into life
I've held you in my arms
kissed you on your forehead
day in day out
I felt you nesting in my chest
how much you loved me
for being caressed and not suppressed
surprised you'd grow under my wings
under my love and under my presence
oh — writing you, my dear book
has been the scariest thing I've ever done
writing you, has been the most
impossible dream I've ever followed
to believe in you before you existed
without the proof I was ready
to take care of you

to let go of who you
were going to be
— you were always
inside of me
and now I'm holding you
in my hands
all of your words
and all of your sentences
you feel so real,
you feel so calm
thank you —
for showing me home

xx elise.

a deep breath before I start
one moment, another moment
opening the doors of my heart

swimming away
from a life lived in vain
it is all an illusion —
my life is an illusion
the pain that lives in my body
shouts at me through my neck
it burns me and it stings me
it refuses to be washed away

what if I go beyond
scratching the surface
because I've scratched
the surface for far too long
what if I go deep into
the essence of my feelings
so deep I can catch pearls
laying on my inner ground
what if I can find those pearls
and happen to see —
mighty glimpses
of my identity

and even strangers
will tell me — who I am

isn't it strange, you look at me and
you see a being — it is strange
you look at me, yet I am not
who you are seeing

if you need me
I'll be at Lost & Found

can someone tell me
where to find my manual
— I am at a loss

did I leave a window open
through which the winds of uncertainty
have managed to find me?

confusion —
the only thing
I'm really clear about

putting my mind to bed
"sleep tight, my little worries"

a few words
lifting the veil of
my inner peace

you keep on invading my zone
you blast into it and take over control
I don't like it — I don't like at all
how you use your pain to get through my wall
can't you see you're pushing away
my blessed state of calm

I want to feel silence
hold peace in my hands
I want to be as light as the wind
dance freely over blessed lands

thrown into the wind
blown to the east,
to the west
into the depths
of my chest

richness buried in silence
it's for me to find
on the doorstep of my heart
far away from my mind

did I leave a window open
through which the winds of uncertainty
have managed to find me?

confusion —
the only thing
I'm really clear about

putting my mind to bed
"sleep tight, my little worries"

if you talk to me
in the language of pain, shame
and blame — I will not listen

I am not your wish list
you cannot add your desires to me
have me tick them off

you are angry with me
well, not the real me
the fictitious me
the one acting she isn't good enough
not talented, lovable, capable

balding your fists —
nodding your head impatiently
I can see you thinking, hurting
wanting to protect me
from me

you make me feel so uncomfortable
you push me, pull me, poke me
until I move, until I change
until I fight — for myself

oh, how I thought
you were attacking me
but now I can see
you were removing
a bullet — hurting
me so deeply

in my essence
I'm so fluid
I'm not an hour
not even a second
the same

so convinced
I am not good enough
when you tell me I am
I feel a glimpse of hope arising in me
and suppress it immediately

I've been searching for the wound
wiggling my finger into it —
pressing on it
until I can let the pain out
the pain needs to get out

I can't carry
no — no longer
the weight of not
being good enough

chasing and hiding behind
shiny people and objects
searching for myself
in the reflections of others

pretty, polished and polite
I say thank you, smile and act kind —
how much longer will I hide
how I truly feel inside?

problems on your plate
— I can see them, feel them, hear them
I silence myself and soften your pain
in darkness I shine a light on you
dim mine along the way

I can feel your pain, misery, stress
a person holding a dam together with bare hands
but the water is already flowing through it
and I am afraid —
afraid that if I speak, the dam will break
and everything you are clinging to will
flow away at high speed
and so I tell you, "it's me — I'm the one who
can't breathe", "I'm the one who needs to be free"
and I leave, I leave you in the unknown
choosing to not set you free

melancholy, melancholy
staring through the rear mirror
into my being

was joy taken away from me
or did I let it slip out
of my being?

today I feel like
a moon without a night
a cloud without a sky
a tree without a forest

the old me
is fiercely disagreeing with
the newly awakened being

on some days
my being is constructed
in a polarised way
everything in me clashes —
like a thunderstorm
on a sunny day

judgments passing
through the sky
dimming the light
i need to see
what it means
to be me

help me —
I'm drowning in a sea
of other people's energies

the danger and the gift of me
is that whatever I touch or see
dissolves into my being

when I'm with you
I feel everything I'm afraid of
it takes every ounce of my being
to stand in a room with you
— act like nothing's going on

"are you sure?"
the embag around
the heart

healing in water
inhaling love, exhaling peace
wondering how long it takes

three little diamonds
rolling down my skin, my heart
— now overflowing

oh, how much you love this game
but I refuse to prove myself to you
be tricked into your winning and losing
needing a trophy to show that I'm worth it
if you truly see me — you will let me be

no need to pretend
between me and you
there is no beginning
no middle — only an end

where are they —
my boundaries

———————————————

my boundaries
seem to be made of elastic
if I want to — I can stretch them for you
all the way to the moon

a safety so dangerous
it keeps me fixed in my place
locked into my ways
and as life passes me by
I never got to understand
when or how
I never said goodbye

staring through the keyhole
in front of what I know is the right door
who is going to let me in?

I go to bed, asking myself
"how do I stay calm when I know
it's time to move on?"
I wake up, asking myself
"how do I move on when I know
I have to stay calm?"

shadows of the past, the old hurts that last
buried in the dark and cool cellars of my body
will I hold onto them or will I let them go?

looking back at the past
I see a door locked and blocked
my cold and shivering hands
holding the key to things I fear
I'm not sure I want to see

one step to the left
one step to the right
moving around my mind
blocking my sight

swimming around you
in circles, squares and triangles
I'll never get closer
I'll never get away

solitude, dear solitude

you are so good
to me

caught up in my mind
I have become
numb to life

afraid to leave this place
to discover tomorrow
this was a mistake
yet I want to grow
I want to know
part of me wants to stay
part of me wants to go

life —
give me a sign
show me I'm moving forward
not behind
show me you're helping me
to unfold my wings
that you have my back
might I be falling

"my dearest mind,
stop controlling
my heart,
let go — it's safe
I promise

"I have a dream", whispers my heart
"that is my fear", shouts my mind

leave a little room for stardust
to create its magic

I will take on my responsibility
to trust, believe and see
there is so much inside of me
that deserves to be set free

no darkness
could overshadow
the light in me

afraid of the words
I'm afraid of the hurt
my words might cause you
of what my truth might force you to do
but if I do not speak out—
free myself from all this doubt
secrets will live a life of their own
in my body and in my soul
a price I'm not willing to pay
because this is my temple
my place of peace, my holy ground
within it nothing but
love to be found

you want the best for me
but the best for me
has to include your being

of course I want you
— but not at the cost
of losing myself

whispers of truth
have been there all along
but somehow I waited
because, what if I was wrong
I found so many reasons
as to why I wasn't ready
took a path that wasn't
safe nor steady
lost in the outer noise
didn't realise
what I didn't trust
was my inner voice

outer limitations
their purpose for me is
to turn my vision inwards

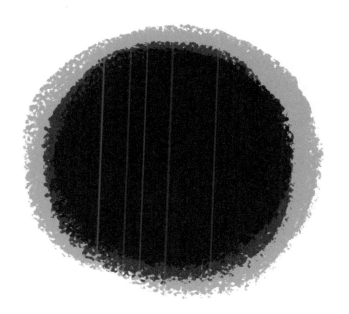

I can't see what's in front of me
but maybe that's just what I need
a bit of darkness to help me feel

cleaning up my inner space
by removing every trace
of my self-protective identity
allowing me to see
all I've been looking for
is already inside of me

I want to be with me, with all that I see
I want to find ways to express what I feel
honour the life flowing through me

each one of us carrying
our little big world inside
seeing it through our own eyes
thinking it through our own minds
feeling it through our own bodies
expressing it through our own stories
all of us learning different lessons
oh, the wisdom of humanity
it's everywhere around me

who will ever know
who will ever understand
how it feels to be me?

I can't live my life
as if I'm sure
I'm going to be here
for a while

instead of guidance
you bring obstruction
block all the turns
I'm meant to take

if I'm not allowed
to make mistakes
to take unknown pathways
how am I ever going to grow
how am I ever going to know
what's beyond the correctness
of this life?

be brave, be bold
take risks, believe in gold
  don't ever be discouraged
  go ahead and have faith
    in your own truth

could you please, at least
open one door in your mind
— look at it from this side?

why take the pattern of the past
predict it's going to be like that in the future
why do that to myself — it's far too limiting

I keep on resisting
possibilities popping up
in my mind yet I
keep on resisting —
who is this I
who is this I that keeps on
locking me inside?

how
a bit of sunshine
makes me see
how
much dust
has been covering
my inner being

all of the cants, shoulds and musts
covering my soul in layers of dust

my insecurities
leading me into darkness
— it's not safe here, is it

"this is it — this is it!", my heart tells me
"but I don't understand", my mind tells me

thoughts
crossing my mind
thunderclouds
in a bright blue sky

am I living the life that is right for me
or right for everyone around me?

standing at the intersection of life
seeing all of these signs:
'what does life want me to live?'
'what life do I want to live?'
'what do other lives want me to live?'

love it,
accept it,
be with it,
appreciate it
don't take it
for granted
the minutes
seconds
of your life

I will go wherever
the moon touches my heart
stars illuminate my mind and
I dissolve into liquid magic

sitting down
taking a deep breath in and out
worries falling out of my head
and onto the ground

this dining table
makes me feel so
loved and protected

I owe it to life
to growth and to evolution
to keep on trying new things
to fully experience what it means
to be a human being

who's in charge?
of course — it's the heart

dim your mind
let your heart decide
when the time is right

growing older yet feeling younger
time must be moving backwards

— through me

laughing out loud
chasing little raindrops
falling from the clouds

a deep longing
to be near the sea
in the midst of the forest
on top of the mountain
a deep longing
to hear waves echoing through my being
to learn from the wisdom of trees
to see new perspectives from mountain peaks
oh — what more do I need
than this realness, this trueness, of nature
teaching me everything on how to be
the fullest version of me

breathe,
fill your lungs
with oxygen
be yourself
flap your wings
in freedom
do what you dream
of doing
stop accepting
what's accepted
question all the answers
find your own ways
live your life
— and make the
most of it

I thought life had its ways
of rubbing wind in my face
now I realise it was me —
walking in opposite ways

what if I see myself
as this bundle of energy
no face, no clothes, no identity
would I then feel more free
to go wherever I need to be?

life as a question mark
somehow it makes much more sense
to leave all full stops and exclamation marks
invite in this wondrous silence

you ask me
"what brings you here?"
I smile
place my hand
on my heart

when I laugh
when I cry
the floor of my heart
bounces

oh I feel called to write
to let this inner creativity
be written to life

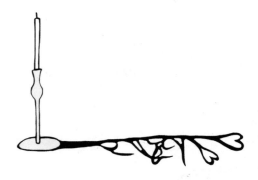

in the shadow of the candlelight
these words will begin to transform
everyone who's open to them —
to the words that touch the soul

when freedom
offers you it's
helping hand
— will you take it?

in the rush of transformation
slowing down to be aware
taking in all these little changes
the being here instead of being there

even the choices
I didn't think were choices
turned out to be choices after all

how can I move forward
from a place of lack
how can I move forward
from a place of non-acceptance
how can I move forward
from a place of revenge
I'm not really moving forward
I'm going back in time

sun
show me
my strength
to rise up from
the ground
let me shine forth
your light

as the sun is moving through my body
shining with love, making me glow
it's whispering to my wounds —
"take your pain with you, it's time to go"

am I brave enough
to speak with the judge
who's breaking down
the wonders in me

don't erase me, replace me or perfect me
appreciate me in my imperfect state
this is where I speak with utmost honesty
where my words carry the most weight

to earth
my dear heart
belongs

it didn't work for me
living life under your lead
I have to go my own way
I have to go, no — I can't stay
even if I don't know where I belong
or where it is that I'm going
I have to be free —
I have to live life in a way
that pleases me

where does the wind
find the bravery and desire
to keep going on and on and on
is it never too tired to climb higher
too weak to wake up at dawn?

what if I can make it?
what if the universe rewards me
for pushing through, for letting go
for trusting in what feels good?

There's a strength
inside of me
covered by a dusty layer
of fragility

when I let go of things that don't matter
block out the unimportant chatter
I know that it is me — I am
going to set myself free

"I cannot hold this dream on my own"
my heart begs my mind

sitting here and crying
finding it oh so frightening
all the things I'm putting aside
to follow the vision I have in mind

a transition point in life
it's easy to believe
this is not the right direction
since it's causing all this friction
the transition is peeling and healing
a big old wound
no I shouldn't
pack my bags with old dirt
as it'll cause me much more hurt
I want to move forward
leave the past behind
let my heart be my guide

rippling through the water
a tiny wave, a big change
crashing inside me

old foundations crumbling down
I feel lost and shaken to my ground
life is asking me to move away
stretch the foundations
of my inner being

witnessing death and
birth at the same time
I find myself standing
in the middle of the
fragility of life

dear life,
what if I'm wrong
will you be there
for me?

tell me —
what weighs up to death
it's life, isn't it?

where to go, where to stay
heart — shew me my way

the sun is shining
my soul is singing
maybe it's time to go
maybe it's time to flow
let my being be taken
by life's divine flow

a summer breeze
slowly blowing life
into my being

I am everywhere and nowhere,
nowhere and everywhere

grey clouds
are bursting
rain is pouring,
blessing earth
now everything grows

it's through this pain
I find it so difficult to write
I'm out in the storm
unprotected

I feel tired, sad, powerless
I'm drowning in the pain of my heart
it pulls me down with it
I can't breathe — I can't breathe
there is so much tension inside of me
please tell me
how can I be free

I keep on writing
writing, writing, writing
since it's the only way
I can stop myself
from being so frightened

how much of the air I breathe

isn't used to speak the truth

hiding in my being?

words can't flow
out of my frozen
being

do I really
not know my truth
or am I deeply
blindly deeply
afraid of it?

my voice —
where are you?

a jungle in my mind
how do I free myself from
mental chatter oh so wild?

oh so wild, the mind
why don't I listen — a song
for me to unwind

do I really, truly,
deeply understand
and embrace —
the freedom in
my freedom?

wandering the pathless woods
taking every step as it comes
following sunshine in darkness
decisions aren't right or wrong
they just give me a different view
on my way home

all you need to do
is what feels good to you
and your life will change
in so many profound ways
you can't even believe
it's this simple
to live your life in a way
that for you only
is just about perfectly
magnificently right

Standing in the forest
as calm as I can be
I can hear the wind
rustling through
the pines —
bringing me back
to me

in the midst of the forest
drifting off in a sensory bliss
slowly unwrapping
nature's gift

river flowing through my mind
I can taste pines in my mouth
this is what nature does to me
it takes me over, loud and proud

older, taller and wiser
than I'll ever be
more forgiving, loving
and patient
dear tree, let me hug you
and kiss you
and I'll release the old
stories residing within me

in the midst of the dark forest
glimpses of sunshine — painting
shadows of leaves on me

admiring the trees
the air and the water
"don't forget yourself"
you whisper in my ear
"you're part of nature too"

what if,
my heart
can't hold out
any longer
to be brave?

just when I think I'm back in control
something beneath my feet slips away
it wasn't so stable after all

life's teaching me again
to not surrender to the thoughts
playing tag in my head

some lessons I learn each day
some lessons I learn once and never again
some lessons I never need to learn
for their wisdom is innate

in the midst of an invisible storm

don't know what feels right and what feels wrong

until I put my pen to paper and realise

my passion is here and it is strong

early mornings
late evenings
in darkness
I shine bright

maybe I should feel loved,
honoured, valued
for the one who is always
here to see my work
the one who is paying attention
from the front row of my mind
is my inner critic who cares enough
to be here every day and every night
every step of the way
she pays attention to whatever
it is that I create
and so I think, deep down inside
my inner critic must love me

I am
the stillness
in the eye
of the storm

like a rock in water
I block my own flow
focus on the bad
the future could hold
like waterfalls, sea storms,
whirlpools...
oh no — how can I let go?
how can I trust that I am strong enough
to ride the unknown?

what the ego wants, the ego gets
but what the soul wants, oh —
please, don't ever forget

what if I let go of
everything that I consider mine
how much of me will be left behind?
how much inner wealth will I find?

my desire is great to have and to hold
but how do I expect to grow
if I never move on —
if I never let go?

stop holding up walls
that are meant
to be torn down

everything I cannot change
why not stop to control
why not let it all go

here I am
holding up the paper
right in front of me
writing to stumble upon
the truths
hiding in my being

my mind — conquered
by a storm of worry

how is it that my mind, my very own mind
part of my flesh, my blood — limits me
with beliefs that aren't even mine?

how do I cut myself loose
from restrictive and suffocating rules
like handcuffs, wrapped around my truth

"what are you doing?"
asks the mind to the heart
"scratching off the labels
glued onto me"

the walls I've put up around me
are here to protect the hurt of past's wounds
it's easier to hold them up than to let them down
at least, that's what I tell myself

hiding from the world
because I can't see my worth
why not show the real me –
open my heart, be vulnerable,
be free

I want, I want, I want —
why not surrender
to what is
why not accept
make the most of
what I've got
— why ignore
make excuses
ask for more

on some days
I live, feel and breathe
a sense of lack
oh, how guilty I feel
when I fail to see
the abundance of life
within me

autumn leaves
dancing like birds
in the sky on
how blessed I feel
to be alive

tune into life
there is so much to write
life is so rich, why deny it —
because it's not what I wish?
imagine if I could let go of that want
life could become my confidant

trust inspiration will come —
when you least expect it —
or, it will make itself known

when you are gifted
with whatever you have
pass it onto someone else
for it is yours to share
when a cloud holds
too much water
it drops it onto planet earth
so that everything on it
can grow

pregnant with inspiration
letting it grow into its form
I trust that when the time is right
this creation will be born

oh, inspiration — an invitation
to creation, I'm here to drink its flow
who knows when it will end its show

awake at night
memories popping up
like little enemies

this hurt
makes me wonder if
it's part of who I am
— how else could it
keep on finding me
wherever I am

it's easier to blame you
for how I am feeling
than to look at myself
open my heart and turn
the pain into healing

truth is
I could never blame you
for the lessons
I need to learn

a silent embrace
by the wind
makes me feel
so loved
and cherished

what if I give my life
to the sun, the stars and the moon
the wind, the trees and the mountains
the water, the air and the clouds

dear tree
do you fear the wind?
why should you, with such
deep roots — it looks like
you're dancing with it

two parts in me
one who deeply enjoys
to be and to stay
one who dreams
of places far away

just like the tree
I drop my leaves
let go of what
doesn't serve me

why did I think I was
in charge of the words
the creation, the inspiration
the only thing I'm in charge of
is not resisting —
wilfully, selflessly, step aside
invite wonders to arise

passion, true passion
flowing through my body
rising up to my chest
heating up everything inside of me
a passion that in its purest form
doesn't care about
who, what, where, how and when
it just comes and it goes
it comes and it goes

dipping my pen
in your emotions
— may I inscribe
your soul
with a love poem?

sitting here
in the midst of the night
catching rays of divine light

this is the moment
I've been waiting for
the moment in which
my life is going to change
asking me to surrender
to go with the flow
courageously, move away
from the place that has opened
my entire being

saying goodbye
to all this richness, just because
of this feeling deep inside
will I be wrong or right —
I guess I'll never find out
if I don't let go now

united by silence
our eyes hold the same apart/lue
the love of being awake
at these early hours

my heart is paper-thin
I can feel your loneliness
tearing me apart

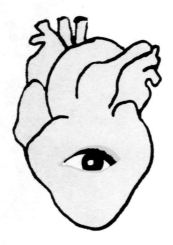

I do not want to not love you
I do not want to not forgive you
I do not want to not talk to you
but at the same time I don't know how
to protect myself when you're around
and so I stay away from you

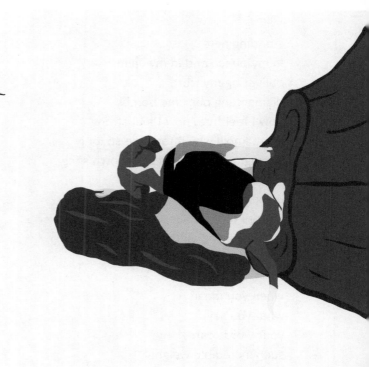

isn't life
just beautiful
to watch

do you ever feel this inner urgency
to breathe — since you are breathing now
to hear — since you are hearing now
to see — since you are seeing now

standing here
in my peace and in my calm
delivering my truth
dismantling our time bomb
now I feel free, now I feel strong
don't know why it took me so long
to sing to the rhythm of my own song

listening to the
echoes of my voice, now —
who's making all this
courageous noise?

when you mean
what you say
your words carry
such incredible weight

up and down
and up and down
my being fluctuates
like the waves
in the ocean

today I choose
me — me — me
and I will be
free — free — free

following my heart
never thought of it as
an act of rebellion

I find it scary to tell you that I'm leaving
to tell you, "no longer can I stay"
how will you respond
will you cry or will you shout
will you be silent or leave no tear behind
I don't know — but what I know is this
I have to move away
I have to follow my heart
trust in my own being

nobody has done it before
but then — at the same time
nobody has been me before

so much perfection
running through my blood
why can't I see that what I do
is so ingeniously good?

— struggling with perfection
maybe I fail to see
the beauty of imperfection

does the bird listen to its voice
doubt if it's a song or just noise?
does the tree look at its leaves
worry about when they'll leave?
does the sea feel its waves
hurt when they move away?
or is nature perhaps perfectly content
with whatever it creates

just like the moon
my light shines bright
when I'm on my own

this lifetime is about me
my dreams, my wishes, my desires
I am the one who's destined
to surrender to my heart's whisperings
it is me — my life has always been about me

on the gloomiest day of the year
when the sea pours out of the sky
and a world of worries inundates my mind
I will find a field of grass
stand in complete silence
spread my arms wide open
invite cold drops of rain to
kiss my skin, and listen
to my heart overflowing

don't expect me
to be the same
in spring, summer
autumn, winter

oh — if only
I'd allow myself more often
to tap into the field of freedom
behind my self-imposed restrictions

surrendering now
time and stillness passing by
— goodbye, my worries

breathe, feel my heart beat
love, let my heart speak
— it glows, a power so deep
nothing touches nor distracts
my peaceful being

how little I need
abundance lives within me
kisses of freedom

the freedom
of being content
with this little,
this much
of life

gifted
minutes, hours, days of sun
at the time of my life
when everything feels grim

I cannot let myself down
when it goes wrong the first time
I trust this is part of the game
of how I'm meant to be playing

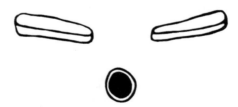

my mind — a pinball machine
kicking around the good thoughts
preventing them from falling into dark holes

I can hear the rain
singing in silence

when the bird discovered its wings
it realised it didn't have to stay in the same place
it could be flying free instead of standing still
use the wind to its advantage

so will you now surrender
— to the magic of this world
have trust and be tender
fly free as a bird

stretching my arms
like the wings of a bird
breathing in deeply
the magic of this world

oh — the weight
on my shoulders
why don't I put it down
on the ground
experience all of this
now warm
freedom

life, come to me
blow your wind through my body
rush through my veins
my heart, my lungs and my brain
show me I'm alive and awake

if the sun could sing
what songs would it be singing?
if the shadows could listen
what secrets would they be keeping?
if the clouds could laugh
how much would they be laughing?
if the wind could talk
to whom would it be talking?
if the mountains could love
how much would they be loving?

the pure beauty
of light,
highlighting parts
that before didn't
seem interesting
at all

you tell me I don't need this
and take away all I'm holding onto
"you can do this on your own"
I look at you, now, confused

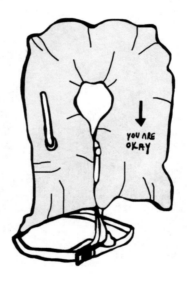

I'm hoping that if you tell me
"it's okay", I'll be protected
I'll be safe

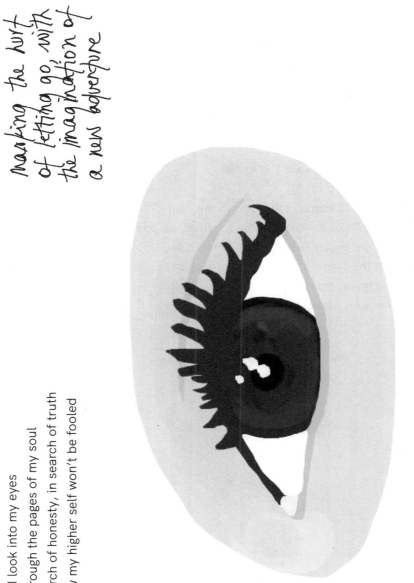

masking the hurt
of letting go, with
the imagination of
a new adventure

when I look into my eyes
flip through the pages of my soul
in search of honesty, in search of truth
I know my higher self won't be fooled

why don't I set free
my talents, gifts, passions
held within me like caged birds

discovering
knowledge and wisdom from within
hearing it, trusting it, letting it all flow —
oh, how empowered I am
by how much I already know

the world in you, the world in me
flying through the universe together, oh so free
wondering what it is we're going to see
is it the night, blessed with a thousand stars?
the trees, caressing each other with their leaves?
the wind, dancing over the fields?

butterfly
oh butterfly
I know — I too
feel so blessed
to be alive

writing is who I am
it's how I live and
how I breathe
writing is not a decision
something I can pause or stop
my life exists in the writing
I am the writing and
the writing is me

would you like a hot cup
of my freshly brewed
inspiration?

oh, the pleasure —
of filling in empty spaces
with my name, voice, handwriting
body, existence

one word — and you turn my world upside down
one word — and I can't concentrate now
one word — and my heart's racing, my mind's chasing
one word — and you turn my world upside down

oh —these daffodils
proudly and boldly arisen
from dark grounds

I didn't ask you
to whisper back to life
the silence in me
but now that you're here
I want to let go of myself
to make sure I'm never
silent again

the sea makes me feel alive
trees calm me down
solitude fills my emptiness
the words I speak are my breath
it's always when I'm out in nature
I feel limitlessly grateful
as complete and as rich
as a human could ever be
there's nothing I need
there's solutions to all my problems
it's the duality of what I see around me
frosty grass covered by warm sunshine
rain on a sunny day
reminding me I don't have to believe
everything I think

show up
— be there
every day
for yourself

within me, above me or around me
there really is nothing to worry about
the sky is always blue so I shouldn't be fooled
when it hides behind a cloud

all these changes
forcing me to trust
myself

oh, this wind
pushing me from the left to the right
from the front and from the back
from wherever it can touch me
it's forcing my roots to grow deeper and deeper
stronger and stronger, longer and longer
until one day — a storm finds me, again
pushes me but I don't move, I don't break
I, gracefully, bend

three doors open
in my mind
through which I might
escape the reality
of life

I feel like
one quarter past
one quarter future
one quarter now
one quarter fantasy

tell me, where
do I draw the line
between fantasy
and reality

mesmerized
by sunlight
creating little
figures on
the wall

it is out of our control
our love for each other
is out of our control
it's flowing
to the moon and back
to the sun and back
to the stars and back
a love as big as the universe
powered by the universe
driven by the universe
multiplied by the universe
a love that's meant to shine
a love that's meant to survive
a love that's meant to be felt
by all of humankind

I stepped outside
entered the darkness,
late at night
wasn't expecting to
be surprised
by the beauty of the moon
shimmering oh so bright

oh, let me be
let me stare into eternity, feel serenity
in this place where time doesn't exist
where beauty is all there is

if I could ever calculate
the vastness of my heart
the love it is able to give
without falling apart
I think I would be amazed
completely blown away
by the dimensions
of my heart

my heart
broken many times
this is me giving you my heart
without feeling like
it'll fall apart

opening the doors of my heart
letting everyone, even strangers
take their part
oh — it feels so good to share
it feels so good to care
to be in this love, together
now and forever

sky's beaming with love
the sun's moving through me now
— it's time to let go

tears travelling down
my skin, kissing me goodbye
old thoughts, I am free

I need to heal
are it is bright
a stig so clear
a shy or blue

do I love myself enough
to walk away from the pain?

I've been here once too often
in this place where I love people
more than they can hold inside

one change after another
growing pains in my heart

today, I feel like
a rose in full bloom

the wind, reminding me of your love
travelling so fast, it comes and it goes
— but will it last?

separated yet so close
it makes me wonder about
a special bond
an invisible cord
strapped around your heart
strapped around my heart
forever together, never ever
not by distance, not by time
not by disease, not by the mind
to be broken apart

I long to feel
my skin against yours
let my heart pick up
the rhythm of yours

I can feel your love
penetrating my skin
like a key unlocking
my heart, guarding
you now, ever more

I could hear
my heart shatter —
into a million pieces

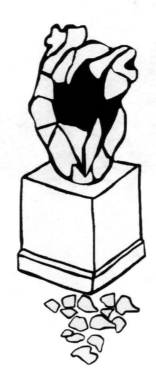

a shattered heart, now
be gentle, be kind — it will
heal but take your time

this sense of stillness
of gratefulness, of peace
is feeding my heart
at its most vulnerable
corners

this is who I am
why hide or even change
what I can't accept — yet?

what if I'm hiding
what someone else
is looking for?

this is who I am
accept me, respect me
please — don't change me

I've come here barefaced

nothing to cover my skin

a freckled story —

I no longer want to hide

or even rewrite

the stars in my night

I want to love, now

this constellation

of me and my ancestors

you make me see
I have to strip away all the unnecessary
fill this space with the essence of my being
you make me see that all I need to hear, feel and see
me, is enough — me, is all I need

am I losing my mind
or am I just about
perfectly
right

is it me, am I really seeing
the entire world
as a completely different being?

the way you love me
makes the question
if I can love myself
more

can I hug myself
the way I hug you?
can I listen to myself
the way I listen to you?
can I care for myself
the way I care for you?

I know we're not in a useless fight
you being here is a hopeful sign
the proof that my body is doing just fine
because of the hurt, the hurt that heals
I can't judge you for how you make me feel
even though I feel so weak
even though I can't sleep
I can't be mad at you
I can't be mad at me
I can only surrender to the beauty
that is a woman's body

do I know
the roads in my body
have I ever desired to go
on a journey through the curves
it's a question that's been puzzling me
'am I giving myself what I deserve?'

why do I keep on going until
my body collapses, it shouts
— it's been enough

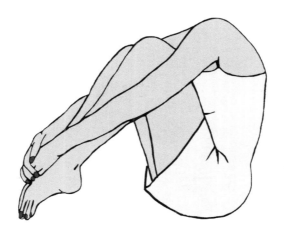

my precious body —
a thunderstorm's rolling in
hurting yet healing

how am I going to be liked
by everyone
how am I going to be liked
by me

if I could get married to myself, would I?
would I stand by my side, in good and bad times?
would I peacefully adapt to my changing ways
manage to make this marriage work
even if I didn't feel nor see hope in my face?

the wind
slowly wrapping
its arms
around my heart

when was the last time
I silenced my fears?

"I am safe"

when was the last time
I valued myself?

"I am valuable"

when was the last time
I loved myself?

"I am loved"

when I look into my eyes
I can sense the pain in my heart
years and years of giving love
to everyone feeling unloved
I've allowed them to use me and consume me
up to the point where I feel heartbroken myself
how much longer will I give my love away?
how much longer will I live without loving myself first?

so short of love
I can see it in my eyes
I can feel it in my soul
dear me, why don't you take
all of my love — tomorrow
I'll be back to bring you more

one cup of self-love, please

how much longer will you take away
love, from others, love
you never gave to yourself

today I feel numb
today I can't see
my mind is too square
and my life feels too real

all I want is to be hugged
so deeply until my pain
transforms into love

falling apart
doesn't mean -
it will break

how do I know what true love is —
how it feels and how it tastes?

my hopes, my expectations
higher than the mountains
higher than the sky

secluded in silence
the only sounds I can hear
— birdsong, wind, water
the essence of nature
the sensuality of life

the one I can talk to
the one that makes me
want to be a better person
now you're gone, out of reach
and it hurts, all over my body
so much that when you're back
I'm reminded of all I've been missing
and so I take you — all of you
as much as I can

seeing your face
I forgot how much strength
and joy you radiate
hearing you talk
I forgot how much your voice
makes my heart all tender and soft

walking in silence, I can feel
the warmth of your skin — oh
I'm about to give in

bt— how you've
captured my soul/
how can I ever
— no never
let you go?

the love I feel for you
I will not — I cannot
let it escape from my heart
oh no, these sparkles of fire
I will hold them against my chest
embrace them with desire
I don't care if they burn me
if they scar my heart
I will not let you take away
my love for you —
not when it keeps me
this warm

when everything in life changed
the floor beneath my feet disappeared
fear took over and forced me to realise that
what I called home wasn't built on solid ground
and wasn't mine to begin with
I had to rearrange myself and my life
dust off my shoulders, heal my wounds
take a deep breath
seek for and gather the elements I could trust
pieces that could build a sustainable home
that would feel like home, remind me of home
even though it was not a real home
because home is a place
where I feel I belong
it's a sweet spot in my heart
that can never be taken away
not by anyone —
not even by myself

today I will say
and I have come
a long way —
I love all of me

oh — how much I'm appreciating
the silence, the peace, the harmony
that comes with finding my place
with accepting my being

through writing I live my life
is how I feel most alive
to express who I am and what I feel
in as many ways as possible
is why I exist, is how I live
a gift I wish to share with you
so that you, too, are not alone
on your way home

journal

2018 - 2022

for months I wrote in my journal
about a soul that
wanted to speak, longed to be
free. so often this writing ritual
ignited a poem. this is the source
the magic behind all.

And then, I disappear. Every once in a while it happens. Usually, when life starts to overwhelm me and I no longer can move along with its speedy flow. It is then, when I long to catch my breath and be in a timeless space so that I can witness life. It is then, when I long to drop everything out of my hands to be still, to be on my own, to be with me. I cannot talk (about it) when it happens; it just happens. I pull away, dissolve into nothingness. Full-on intro-retrospection mode. And then, a carousel of my past actions, memories and experiences starts rotating in my mind. During such a reflective time I question everything. "Am I on the right path? Am I getting the most out of myself, out of my life, out of my work? Am I surrounding myself with the right people? Are there any habits, thought patterns, people I should let go of?" It is intense to be questioning every aspect of my life. At the same time, I feel blessed by this inquisitive power. These moments in solitary stillness rescued me. Course-corrected me. They changed me in ways I cannot even begin to imagine or put into words.

Oh, I cannot have this. I cannot have people reaching out to me, pulling me out of this solitary stillness when it is yet too early to step out of it. I get snappy. I enlarge distances. I pull away, get even more into hide-mode. But, animals are allowed. Trees are allowed. Sunrises are allowed. Even people passing by (who leave me alone) are allowed. Because, this is my time. My sacred time. No knock on the door, no message on my phone. I want to, need to, be alone. It is where my oxygen is, where my healing power lives. Oh, how I no longer want to apologise for it, explain it, change my behaviour anymore. No longer do I want to step out of this peaceful zone just because someone asks or needs me to. It is a challenge — but I will gladly take it. Dance with it. Because these moments, oh, they carry gold. They allow me to show up in the world with a higher vibration than before. They allow me to show up with fresher perspectives, more energy, clarity. They allow me to be me. They too, are me.

What is it that I am feeling? I know what I am feeling but why am I feeling this way? It is heavy, deep. Not dark but on the edge of disappointment, confusion and melancholy. It is uncomfortable and disorienting. I hear a heavier critical voice than normal. One that judges, holds me back. The voice is evaluating everything. It is a tough exercise to have faith and trust in myself. To see myself. I cannot see myself today; who I am. I am confused about who I am. I cannot really see the strengths in me. I am worried. Worried that I do not matter, that my work does not matter. It is these kinds of soul-tumbling feelings that are hanging over me like shadows or dark clouds. They destabilise my being. They distract me. And I know: it is not real. This is my mind. So why am I thinking, feeling, it? It is difficult to be focused now. It makes me look for confirmations, answers, consolations...

I want to appreciate chaos. To be calm in confusion. I want to feel peaceful. Even, especially, when I feel this inner restlessness. When not everything is at its designated place and I feel so out of control or have no clear overview of the situation. For the sake of my own health, I need to let go. Now. Appreciate disorder. Like in a forest, where there are lots of different plants, trees, weeds. It is still beautiful and peaceful to be there. Could I trick my mind into believing those two are the same?

What a beautiful sunset walk... It happened like this: I sat on the couch, half asleep, listening to the wind calming my mind. Suddenly, a beam of sunlight hit my face. Oh, I cannot tell you how that made me feel! I started glowing from the inside out and I knew what to do: dive into nature. What a good decision. I could breathe again. A big bang: windows opened in my head. I heard birdsong and noticed the sky. Oh, so magical. A blue sky with soft pink clouds. It said, "And now we thank you for being so patient in the storm." I loved it; I loved how the warmth of the sun made the scents of the forest more intense. I didn't take my usual route but followed sunshine instead. It was, again, such a good decision.

I keep on catching myself in defensive behaviour. What is it with this defensive behaviour? Why does it rise up in my being? What inside of me do I feel is being threatened? Or is this defensive behaviour actually a good thing; a sign of me protecting my individuality, of me wanting to do things my sacred way? I will observe it more closely, see if it rises up again today. Collect some more real-life data. I did notice something else. You know what: it feels like I am floating. Not really floating, but somehow when I observe myself I can see that I am floating in the universe. Not heading into any clear and logical direction. Not walking a tried-and-tested route. Not even setting out a specific course. I am just being me.

Floating. And it feels strangely good. Light. This must be what it means to surrender to something that is bigger than you. To let go of control. To let go of trying to shape your life; of inserting a navigation code.

It is okay to practice. It is okay to make mistakes. I take a deep breath and allow myself to learn. This sentence echoes in my head: "I first have to do it before I can improve it." I am repeating it. "First do it. Do it." Now I feel safe to go again. Humour also helps. I will tell myself: "Elise — laugh. Make it light, playful. Laugh at yourself, at your imperfection, at your humanity." It helps to override my fictitious fear like this. I should not forget to enjoy the process. It is actually quite exciting to witness a process of growth. To see each action as an opportunity to expand. Again, it is okay to experiment. To let go of the pressure of doing it right the first time. It feels so nice to try new things. To learn from what I am doing. Experimentation is the path I am taking and walking.

I am fascinated by humour. The way it so easily lifts spirits and breaks away tensions, frustrations and other limiting weight. It is so important to be able to laugh at myself. With myself. To not only be sad and sobbing in my emotions but to also be able to laugh out loud at and with them. If you manage to find that fine line between humour and misery and dance on it; know it is gold.

I live life at a very intense level. At times, the awareness reaches me of how each human being perceives life in such a different way. That is overwhelming: how we all smell, taste, see, feel and hear differently even though we are in the same space. How is it even possible we understand each other? When I look at myself, oh: there are multiple worlds living inside of me. Obviously, it helps me to get my inner content out on paper. It is good to see it on paper. I am so curious about my life. Do you know that feeling? Curious about the things you will achieve, feeling your own potential… I wonder if someday I will achieve something bigger than my life. If I leave a legacy, something that will be here on earth for years and years after I no longer exist. Perhaps, this book. If yes, then I really hope it is going to be a force for good. It is and has been good for me. Creating this book has been such a valuable process to learn more about myself, my inner workings, limitations, passions. It has changed my life, mind, health…

Writing makes me a more aligned person. In touch with what I feel, think; with how I experience and perceive life. I like feeling this clear, feeling life this deeply. I am grateful for and excited about life blessing me with insights and wisdom the older I get. It is the biggest gift. It is what makes it worth being alive. Each year, I get new gifts of wisdom and growth. New ways to experience life, myself... I used to feel pressure around being or becoming a certain age. Now, I hardly remember how old I am. I am happy to be content with who I am, with where I am and with what I am doing. Isn't it fascinating: all of us living our own lives, having our own ideas about life, wanting the best for our own lives. Isn't it strange: that we are all very much the same in that. All of these separate individuals looking for the same things. Separated because of our uniqueness, united because of our similarities.

A lot of foundations are cracking. It takes all of my energy to remain calm and breathe through it all. I am breathing through a lot. I can see myself struggling to maintain structure, focus and even to have energy. Life in itself, breathing in itself, is enough of a task. I am constantly trying to get myself back on track. But it does not work like that. I cannot force it. I am still coming to terms with life as it is right now. So many flashes of the past are (still) appearing in my head. Most of these memories help me to see how I move through life. I am noticing that the question of "Am I good enough?" still gets to be on centre stage. Have I been like this my entire life? Have I always expected myself to do it right the first time? I push myself too far, too soon, to perfection.

Wounded in my core. Bleeding in my heart. I do not know what is causing it but it is all okay. It is okay if I take it slow today. It is okay that I feel tired because of it. Just take it slow today. I would be grateful to learn new methods of dealing with memories. I feel, at times, that I have no control over them. My skin bares memories; I am able to feel the exact way I felt back then. Sometimes that is not so much fun and other times it makes my heart open so deeply. I am being brought back to the first time I broke away from limitations. I remember being open and unlimited towards myself; about who I was and what I could achieve. I started doing lots of different things, pushed through fear and motivated myself to be bold. I believed in my potential. I achieved 'seemingly' impossible things.

I remember praying a lot. At night in bed, I would talk to something bigger than me. Asking it to guide me, to care for me, to show me the way. Mmm, it felt reassuring.

I do not feel there is space for me on earth. I don't feel anyone needs me. That I am contributing. So why am I here? What is the purpose of me being here? I feel invisible. I do not want to be invisible. I want the opposite: to be seen. Paradoxically, it feels like every day is becoming more valuable and purposeful. Especially since I started writing this book. It is just that I ponder my existence, the value of my existence, from time to time. Every now and then, my heart is tired of jumping hurdle after hurdle. At times, the heart needs to rest. This feeling of loneliness, of lack of support, is what makes me feel invisible, underappreciated. A shadow in the world. Is life meant to be feeling this challenging? Is that normal? Can I make life lighter and more fun? Can I stop worrying, even amidst the biggest of problems? Can I, in a way that's authentic, aligned and joyful for me, make sure that I am safe and supported?

I can bring this wound into the light. I can heal this myself. I can value, see, support and encourage myself, talk to myself, be my own cheerleader. I choose to set free all the inner blockages that prevent me from being free. I deeply trust each moment. My energy in this moment determines the success of the next moment. I know who I am and so, I let go of what other people see in me or think of me. I deeply trust and honour my voice. I speak with confidence and love. My voice holds deep wisdom; it is my best friend. I listen to what it has to say and I trust in what it says. I radiate love, I am love, I share love. When my body is tired, I respond to it with understanding. I will give it the rest it needs. My body deserves to restore itself. When my mind is overflowing, I will respect it. I will respect its capacity to be creative and inspired. On a daily basis, I let creativity speak through me. I will let creativity circulate through my body, open me and release me from all that I feel. I am good at what I do. I work at an intentional and high-vibrational pace. I focus and create with love. I trust the whispers of my heart.

What a magical sunset walk. So many animals came to greet us. First, we saw two horses. I combed their hair with my fingers, looked them into their eyes. We walked on. In the middle of a field, a red kite flew towards us. So close! It was beautiful and it felt liberating. We watched the kite dancing in the sky. We spotted another one, sitting in the field, ready to take off. Another beautiful show. We continued our walk. In the forest, we sat down next to the lake. We watched the sun dip its bottom in it. Soft colours appeared; pinks and yellows. Geese came flying in like hydroplanes. I noticed three little coots in the middle of the lake, calling oh so loudly. I was in love with the scenery. Then, as we started walking again, a deer crossed our path. It jumped so elegantly at high speed and hid itself in the bushes. I felt so blessed to be alive. I could feel life (each and every second of it) in my heart and it tasted so rich. What a blessing to be alive. We continued our walk. As we entered the last meadow, some sheep and one little lamb (which stood proudly on that fallen tree) greeted us. Mmm, what a blissful walk. Now, back home, I sense this delicious peaceful balance. Nature healed me, again. Thank you.

I am on the most beautiful sunset walk. It is incredibly beautiful and silent. The sun is pink. Oh, it's gorgeous. I feel so blessed, replenished, loved by the sun. The sky is milky. Incredibly soft to look at, like a big hug or a big comfortable blanket from the universe. I feel blessed to be witnessing this. I pat myself on the shoulder for taking the time to witness it. This is beautiful. As the sun disappears, it leaves these gorgeous pink stripes in the sky. Oh, so dramatic… Its reflections are caught in the water and its pink hues now touch my face. I feel one with the sunset. What a beautiful day to be alive. To observe deer running away, squirrels climbing trees, birds flying in the sky. It is a sacred experience. I can sense that I am clearing up the space in me. Not allowing myself to think about the past or about the future is helping me. It is clearing up space and time. I mean, there only is the now. If you think about time, it is one continuum. One big pink continuum.

I was born to dance to the tune of my own song. A song that other people cannot hear, for it is my tune. It is okay that I am changing my tune every now and then, that I am changing rhythm every now and then. That is me, that is so me. I wasn't born to worry about things going wrong. Maybe at times; but those worries are meant to be felt only once and then I will move ahead in an even more liberated way. My life is not meant to be fixated on other people's wrongdoings but on our rightdoings. On setting us free from ourselves, from our own judgments and from environments holding us back.

I want to protect and celebrate the individuals in this world. People who feel limited by systems, who cannot go with the flow, who do not have the support of a family or a place they can call home. I want to celebrate them, give them safety, liberty, the right to exist, without labelling them differently. I want to accept them for who they are. Proudly, generously, whole-heartedly. Give them the respect they, too, deserve and need. Because they are human. They, too, should be free — enjoy a life lived in dignity.

I have been cleaning my house. My inner house as well as my brick-and-mortar house. It feels much lighter, brighter. My load has lightened. My environment has a lot of impact on me. I am so fluid in my being that the moment I walk into a space, I absorb a lot. Not necessarily because I want to, but because it just happens. I feel the space so deeply in my core. I feel where it is stagnant, where lives the old hurt, where there is cosiness, joy. Information enters my body and my body starts acting in alignment with it. So, when I bring my surroundings into the alignment that I feel it needs to be, things just start flowing from the inside out. It is mysteriously magical. As a protection mechanism, I have trained myself to ask myself from time to time: "Do I still know and feel where my boundaries are?" It is easy for me to be one with all around me. It is a gift and a challenge. I will manage it in the way that works for me instead of against me.

I feel peaceful today. I love it: feeling like a calm ocean. The sun is shining on my waters, making it shimmer and reflect stronger than usual. I feel vast. I cannot even see where this ocean starts and where it ends. I love it. It is an incredibly soft feeling. I am being hugged by the universe, the world, everything around me and in me. I feel loved, I feel in love, I am love. There is so much softness around me, running through me. I can see it in my eyes: a magical sparkle. My skin looks relaxed. I also have this very deep feeling in my heart. A warm, glowy feeling. It is very, very, open today. It might burst open, so many butterflies in there. I feel untouchable. Covered by a bright and white protective layer. It is so easy to be, delicious to be still and note this emptiness in my head. I can hear everything.
I am so open. Like a very still lake (goodbye, ocean) and every sound is like a drop falling on that lake. Or light like a feather (goodbye, lake) floating in the forest, whispering to the wind: "Take me with you wherever you go…"

I am hearing the call to change. My entire being is resisting. Why can't I go with the flow? Why am I like a mighty rock, not moving at all? Why is it that my being feels like it's losing when it's changing? Like it's cheating on the old when I am changing into new? Why is my being not seeing that staying is preventing me from evolving? You know what: this is the moment. My chance to step away from it all and see what life is presenting me: a boat to step onto. A boat that can take me into a direction that is neither right or wrong. Will I step onto it or will I fold my arms across my chest and resist this change, never to discover and see new ways?

The duality of change. I talk and dream oh so easily and bravely about changing my life... but I am shaking, trembling. Trying to not get usurped by the powers of the mind, of having no answers, of giving my all to faith and to surrender to that feeling in my heart. I know this is life. This is growth. I take a new step and I have to level up energetically. I have to let go of old things that do not serve me any longer at this stage. When you know what you want to do and it scares you, you have to pull out all of your courage and still do it. If you really like it, you still do it, even though it is so incredibly confronting. Even though it makes you feel vulnerable. This inner urge to change teaches me to let go of old stuff that weighs too much and pulls me down with it. It confronts me with my mental limitations.

This is not me being unsure about a decision. This is me experiencing the emotions that go with transitioning. Sometimes transitioning is easy, sometimes it is hard and I feel miserable about the unknown. My being loves the comfort of holding on, it does not (yet) naturally appreciate the art of letting go. It is more like an octopus with its eight arms gripping the walls of the comfort zone. I can see it from a higher viewpoint: I am riding a rapid river and I am in this in-between-zone. The pressure is building up, I am almost ready to ride. Then I remember: I am in for the ride. I have always been in for this ride! So, let's go.

"Just do it: find a tree and write next to it." As I look into her crystal blue eyes, she delivers me (my) truth. A delicate but firm reflection. I cannot hide, the way she looks at me as we are sitting here on the bench, I just cannot move with (my) truth in between us. I cannot do anything but transform, let go of my old story. Rewrite it, now. I'm lost for words yet so relieved. She is right. The way I have been doubting my identity, my sense of direction and my desires with these questions... It's been preventing me from tapping into my sense of direction. Only a few minutes ago I was asking myself: "Am I weird for wanting to write in the forest? Am I strange for feeling like truth comes to me in a clearer way when I'm in the forest?" Not even realising the first thing: that I knew I wanted to write in the forest. But her eyes. Oh, her eyes... And the way she delivers the message to me; so calmly, gently, lovingly. I feel protected. Encouraged. It is the encouragement my heart didn't know it needed to hear and I am deeply moved by it.

Weeks later, I am still deeply impacted by that one encounter. It did not matter that I hardly knew her. Her words touched my heart. They became engraved in my mind. And whenever I want to, I replay that sentence in my head as it nudges me into the right direction: "Just do it. Find a tree and write next to it." I am so glad for having opened up about it. Since then, my life has started to change. From writing in a fixed and controlled way behind my desk (feeling like everything 'had to be just in the right place' for me in order to write) to me being free, needing nothing more than a pen and paper. From then on, I have been writing in lots of different places. Experimenting with what comes up on my pages, how it changes, how it stays the same. I have been writing next to trees, the lake, on top of mountains, in the big city. Wherever I am, now, the moment I feel inspired, I catch it on paper. And it makes me laugh, every time again. To me, that is success. That is going with the flow, letting go of my boundaries and truly being free.

It's getting darker. The transition from dark to light (or from light to dark) speaks to my soul. Sitting here behind my desk, I can see the sky being a deep blue with a soft orange bottom. Whatever it means 'to be a writer': I feel like that now. Like someone being dedicated to her life's work. I like that person, I like me, I like being me. Now it is dark. Oh, I love the dark. I can feel the energy slipping away... things getting calm and silent around me. I feel guided, loved. A message comes my way: to enjoy every step along the way. It does not matter what or how I do what I do — it is right. Two more messages come my way: "You cannot really lose that much if you yourself are still here; healthy and alive. Give importance to the right things. Value the life within you more than everything around you." I will listen to my voice, to my heart. When I give my fullest attention to that which is in front of me, the next step will unfold when the time is right. Trust each step, trust the timing. I do not need to hurry. I only have to follow my heart and my sense of direction. It is not scary. I know how to do this; I have always known how to do this. I trust that I will figure it out when I do not (know). I can do this on my own, I understand that I am capable and strong — especially when challenged.

When the mind kicks in... the feeling of surrender can feel so frightening. Not in an anxious way, but in a 'wow I don't know where my life is guiding me' way. It can feel overwhelming: the not knowing. Thoughts run through my mind, trying to grab my attention, saying: "But Elise, where is the proof? What can we hold onto? How can we trust in something bigger which we can't even see?" The underlying question here, of course, is: Is life taking me anywhere? Should it be taking me anywhere? I do know this: I feel like I am standing at a crossroads and I am letting go of control over where to go. It is so different from how I have lived my life before. This, 'let it unfold and I will follow whatever feels good', is so new to me.

It just happens. People projecting themselves onto me. A lot, lately. Telling me who I am, what I should or should not say or do. When it happens, I cannot always look at the situation from a higher point of view. When it happens, I am in it. Oh, I feel it... Allowing myself to feel is healthy. It is healthy, human, to feel both joy and pain. I do not want to go back to being a concrete wall (I couldn't, even if I tried to), back to being someone who is covering up her sensitivity because "that is how you lead." Pushing away the sensitivity, the purity, of a human is dangerous. It is not healthy to act like you are untouched by all that life brings you. At least, not for me. I can feel joy so much more deeply because I allow myself to feel pain too. Pain, but also: melancholy, confusion, fatigue. It is not a weakness; it is a pure state, it is truth. It takes courage and strength to feel it. To not want to dissolve it or hide it but to name it, sit with it. Besides, I have learned that it is great input for art. The moment I am sensing a truly uncomfortable feeling, I am actually in the process of creating new art. Life, being alive, is art.

To know myself. Moreover, to hold onto that sense of self without letting it slip out of my hands: oh, it is a life's task. I feel so unstable and confused right now. Lost in it all. I do not know where to go, what to do, what to feel, what to say.

I feel lost in life yet at the same time so clear about life. I find it, quite often, confusing to not see and understand who I am and why I do what I do. But that is the truly wonderful thing about writing: it's a mirror. It mirrors so much of me back to me. It is refreshing, delicious. It is the place where I can truly connect with my sense of self. It is where I come home.

Oh, I feel so light today. Free as a bird flying high in the sky. I sense a big smile inside of me, stretching the corners of my entire being. Oh, I feel like writing today. Mmm. I am experiencing a delicious sensation, the one you get when entering a bakery — that homey feeling. The weather helps too, as the sun is shining but there are some dramatic clouds hanging in the sky. Perfect circumstances to write.

I've got a busy mind. Yet I am appreciating it today. I am letting my thoughts pass by like a slideshow. All of the thoughts, memories, visions. It's a slideshow I did not ask for but one that sure did start playing with me sitting front row. And I have a choice: to be an actor in the play or to watch it from far away. In an attempt to bring myself down to earth, I give my mind an instruction: to say out loud what it is that it sees. And so, whilst walking in the forest, I name all that I see. "I see grass, I see trees, deer, squirrels. I see pinecones and it smells like the trees are breathing summer." Then I wonder: Is it even possible to walk through the forest with an empty mind? To see grass where there's grass, to see trees where there are trees? I wonder how that must feel? To be so clear and empty from within; a clear vessel. To be completely one with your experience. To dissolve those barriers that separate you from the life that's happening in front of you. Through you.

Light, darkness. A play. A dance. I always try to find the exact right time between darkness and light. I love a bit of morning darkness, especially during a morning walk, so that I can experience the rising of the sun. That fills me up in such a deep way. To hear the music of life, its volume being turned up. Crescendo! Or when the sun starts setting, mmm. I don't know how, but I always manage to be out in nature at the right time. It's when life becomes quieter. Softer. Diminuendo. I feel more alive; my senses heightened. The gold in front of me becomes the gold inside of me. No matter how busy (I think) my life is: sunrises and sunsets get priority no matter what. They are what keeps me healthy. They heal me so deeply.

I also love the darkness of the night. That deep-deep darkness. It's my writing juice. It is when I see so clearly and when it becomes so much easier to pour the light out of me. I mean, that stillness... I love it!

Note to self. Dance with life. Because life really loves to dance. The moment I let life guide me on this dance floor called earth, amazing things happen.

I will step out of my home-made box. In my life, I have been called out a lot for being sensitive, vulnerable, doubtful. The way it was being pointed out to me... Words, when spoken with intention, can have an impact on someone's life. For a long time, I thought the impact I felt because of these words were somehow my fault. "I was weak. I had to toughen up. I had to be better." A collection of the ways that I commanded myself. But all that... made me step away from my truest nature. I am my own person. No longer will I let someone's opinion of me become my reality. I am courageous enough to not hide my sensitive heart. To follow my direction instead of seeking direction through everything and everyone around me. Having said that, I am not really clear on where to go next. Maybe now is not the time for me to know. I will let it come to me when the time is right.

I have just experienced a creativity earthquake. One that makes every single body part shake and tremble. One that pulls me into superfocus, makes me forget about everything around me. I wrote and wrote and wrote. I did not judge. I do not know if I was creating quality but I had a lot to say and I wrote it all down as fast as I could. It all just streamed through me in bursts of words. Oh — it was good! To experience this need, thirst, to write and at the same time experience the calm, intensity, purity and the aliveness of being on these pages. It is what centres me; to feel the words flowing through my being straight onto the pages. To experience the flow in me. To open myself up to everything I see. Writing is my way of letting myself know that everything I see, feel, hear or do could be interesting to write about.

Leaves dancing in the sky. This morning, when I sat down behind my desk, I felt this incredible urge to go for a walk. I quickly changed out of my pyjamas and walked into the forest. I felt like absorbing the morning freshness and the intensity of the forest. It is always nice to become aware of how, at the beginning of the walk, it is still all 'think, think'. And then, the deeper I get into the forest, the more it becomes 'surprise, surprise'. I was so impressed by the beauty of the forest, by all of its different colours. The magical shadows between the trees. How the leaves danced in the sky like birds. I stood still, unable to move, wanting to take everything in. At one point, I felt inclined to sit down next to a fallen tree. I like to collect objects during my walks. Pieces of wood, stones. I like to hold them, observe them, feel them. I am impressed by nature's creative intelligence and skill in crafting beauty.

Oh, how I love taking photographs. I truly do. It is an act of creation in which my mind has very little to say and yet it always tries to. Which makes me laugh, because it is almost never right. I never photograph what I intend to. I promised this to myself: to never leave the house without my camera. Even though I might not use it; the carrying it is a symbol. Of observing, appreciating and honouring life, every vanishing second that can never be repeated or relived. I always end up taking a photograph because it just happens. Right in front of my lens, these little divine moments show me that I am doing the exact right thing at the exact right moment. Quite often they (magically) finish the poem I had in mind. "Thank you, nature!" I say and then my entire being lights up. This process is something my mind cannot understand but has to allow to exist and therefore I enjoy it so much.

Oh, nature! Nature and I attract each other in a deep way. As if it calls my name, "Elise, Elise — where are you today, will you come out to play?!" Nature takes good care of me, it really does. I don't know anyone or anything that possesses such power over me. I feel blessed to witness the little wonders of nature. I am closing my eyes now. Witnessing the colours I see with my eyes closed. Different shades of blue, yellow and pink. Peace and abundance wash over me. A poem! I grab my notebook and write it down. Paradoxically, it is about being quiet, calm and focused. A double-layered experience. I can hear the birds singing. I have never heard a bird singing so pure and bright. I smile. My mind wanders. How I love to write by hand. To witness words appearing on paper, words that by no means could have originated in my head since it is the first time I am meeting them on paper. That is what makes this creative process so much fun. I believe it is a blind date between me and the creative potential of the universe.

I feel the changes and choices that I have been making. The last few weeks, months and years are finally paying off. Not that I need them to pay off, I forgot that was part of the game. It definitely feels like I have matured and aged. I have become so much more authentic. True to the voice inside of me, even though I always thought I was authentic. This feels different; grounded yet elevated. It is strange to suddenly be able to feel it. It is my heart's wish to be me, to act like me, to show my boundaries as me, and, at the same time, to feel and respect the other person's way. To be empathic at just the right level and not be overwhelmed by it. It is truly a gift to feel what other people feel. It is my writing juice. It is what I use to write and discover new layers of emotions, of poetical impact. I have to experience but not suffer; that's what is important for me to learn. The right amount of involvement with and detachment from the world of feelings.

Today is such a beautiful day. I am sitting on the sofa, waking up to a new day with a freshly brewed coffee resting on my lap. I am looking at the garden through the stained-glass windows. They are opened and I see and feel the fresh morning wind playing with the curtains. I want to notice every second of the sun increasing its intensity, of how it is colouring the fields of grass almost golden. Oh, I feel so happy to be alive! So happy to awaken amidst all this beauty. To be able to see it, feel it, hear it, smell it. This silence, richness. I am feeling so comfortable, so peaceful. I notice that I am smiling at the birds circling the garden. I do not know why I do that or why they make me happy but they do. Oh, they do… Something about the essence of nature, and life, really, makes me smile from the inside out. Oh I feel so blessed to be alive.

I love pondering, wondering, asking, observing. It is me; I am starting to accept it. As well as my own rhythm, speed, methods and the trial and error I go through. It is all okay. It is all okay. Mmm, I love how I feel now. Energy is here right when you need it; without having to force and push things. Interval-energy, interval-working, I love it.

I am witnessing that life is teaching me to be content with less. In return, it brings me more life-richness. I so love it that I can walk through nature and feel blessed from head to toe. I have had such a beautiful day today. A true spring day. The sun was shining intensely, the sky was powerfully light blue. Oh, it was satisfying to witness. I was impressed by the birdsong. Were the birds, too, celebrating spring? Today, after my walk, I wrote and wrote and wrote. Then I took a hot shower. I felt like being with myself, taking care of myself, give myself the gift of time, peace, attention and love. I am getting better at letting go, at learning that I can live without lots of things. Things are not as important as human beings. First beings, then things. Important to get that order right.

Oh, I feel so much right now. I am ready to pour it all out of me. I have taken time to restore my body, my mind, to get to a place of peace and calm. The inside of my head and body has been a very crowded place for the last few weeks. I kept on ignoring it all. Sleepwalking right through it, hearing it but not doing a thing about it. Bottling it all up. So, today, I did something I do not do often enough: I let it all go. In one big sigh, I let it all go; all of the things I planned on doing. I sat down in nature. At first, I got anxious. "I am doing nothing." My mind started fetching all of these reasons and people telling me I need to be busy. Then I calmed myself again. In that state of calm, a new wave of worry found me. I got a bit sad and melancholic. But then, out of the blue, I entered a place of imagination. It felt nice. I was appreciating everything around me. I looked at the birds feeding their children, at the pink roses covering the wall, at the bees being incredibly busy. "Busy! And I am doing nothing!" my mind shouted and I laughed.

I have been allowing myself to not think in fearful ways. To write with the fear-button turned off. I did not realise it was on, I just noticed I could turn it off. It truly seems to be the main thing that I am learning: to let go of the fear of not being good enough. As if that is the main act in my life's festival: to imagine strange scenarios of all of the bad things that could happen. Why would one be so distrusting, or even afraid, of good things happening? Of actually deserving good? Could it be that I am afraid it will cause me bad luck? Disappointment? Shock? Pain? It is so strange to catch myself in a state of 'bad things will happen to me'. Why would my body, my mind, launch this program? Making me feel the way it does? I have to rewrite this, rewire my mind. I am learning to be comfortable with feeling okay, feeling content, deserving of all the good, being happy, in love with my work. It is my lesson, part of the program of my life's festival.

I've been exploring the must-do's in my head. Noticing when they pop up and not validating them on purpose. Just as an experiment, to see what it does to my energy. So far, I can say it's weird and unusual to be doing something because I feel like doing it rather than having the feeling I have to do it. To invite playfulness back into my life feels frightening. I feel ashamed, embarrassed, on the path of failure... But let me tell you, once I accept it and am in it: it's magic. I thoroughly enjoy it. I love seeing myself like this. When did I stop playing? When did I start believing that playing won't lead me anywhere?

It's a big desire in my life: to invite play. I want to play and I want to see play. Wherever and whenever there is no play (no lightness, no childlike curiosity) a part of me feels disenchanted. What I like so much about play is that it brings out the naturalness in people: their essence. Little Elise would be so proud of me right now. With her optimistic attempt at bringing home ten books from the library-bus to read in one week and her love for special books, she is thrilled to see that now, she herself, is bringing home one big book: her book. Yes: I am on the right path in life. I am being me and I love it.

Do you know that feeling? When you look at someone or something, you just know which way to go? These northern star-beings (people, animals, trees or things) guiding you to wherever you need to be? I truly enjoy it. Wherever I look, there's always a guide. My task is to find them. It's a game I love to play: Spot the Guiding Star. I look around and, "Yes – it must be you!" And I thank it with a joyful heart and smile for showing me where I didn't know I needed to be. That confirms to me: we're all in it together, more connected than we think. I remember the way I once toured England. I said to myself: "No looking at maps; the sun will be my guide." And so, I followed the rays of light for hours and miles. How often I smiled! Gliding through life whilst being held in the universe's arms. That moment is why I am still here. That moment persuaded my heart to be here.

Today is a very rainy day. Rain, a lot of rain. And wind, a lot of wind. They challenge me; the two of them together. It's easy when I'm indoors, because then I feel safe, cosy, inspired. But almost, almost, did the rain-and-wind-duo seduce me to cancel my nature-date. Glad to communicate that I didn't listen: I ignored it and went out.

Because rain + wind is delicious. It blesses you with a mind-and-body wash. And so, as soon as I got outside, I loved it. I puddle-jumped and felt liberated. At first, I felt agitated of course, but that only enabled me to let go even more. And then the forest... The moment I entered it, I felt this deep love and health wash over me. Actually, every time I'm in the forest, the first thought that comes to mind is: "I feel so healthy, thank you." As soon as I got back home I could feel more clearly. I sensed how loaded my mental and physical baskets had been. I was packed with memories, beliefs, experiences, emotions — holding me back, keeping me fixed in my place. I had to let go of them as they formed obstacles in my present. I can't say it's all gone now; it's a long-term recalibration process. But if my body and mind were an ocean, they'd be beautifully calm right now. Perhaps one or two birds flying above the water, trying to catch some fish, might be met by a dolphin jumping high in the sky. Now, I can hear the trees. They're talking, loudly conversing. It sounds beautiful... A pheasant, I can hear a pheasant! How much I love the pheasant's call. Oh, now a small deer is passing by... I'm in complete awe of this moment. What a wonder it is to be quiet and witness life.

I am experiencing a wave of boldness. A courageous moment, in which I listen to myself and hear a voice say: "Be bolder, freer, step away from the shyness, the politeness, the adaptiveness. Break free from it. Dance. Be less afraid to be weird, abstract, to not be understood. This book, this work, this life: it's for me, for me only. And so, the only thing that matters is: do I understand it? Do I like it? Do I resonate with it?" I am now going to write a personal letter of motivation to myself: "You can do whatever you want. This is your book. Make it the way it makes you feel good. Don't be afraid, don't be shy. Show yourself in full glory and whatever you're hiding. Be proud, embrace the life and love within you. This book is yours, make it yours. It won't be taken away from you. It is your love; your heart makes this book shine. Embrace it, wholly, fully, with every body part. No matter how long it's going to take you, walk the road. Take your time. Enjoy it, appreciate it, deeply savour it. Walk the road. Do it. Do it the way you want to do it. Be here, on the paper. Make every poem, every page, your best friend. Give it what it deserves. Love, peace, a beginning, a middle, an end. Time. Give it time. Whatever you feel it needs. Bring and give it dignity, respect. Call the poems into life with all the love in your heart, for they love you too. Each time you give them a piece of your heart, they will flourish, they will grow, they will shine, they will let you know how grateful they are to be by your side. But there is one key thing for this to succeed: focus. Feel grounded. Take the time to be here. Don't be rushed, worried, hurried, pressured. Be patient, be calm. Remember: it may not always come the way you expect it. Trust the unexpected, be surprised, open-minded. Release it the way it wants to be released and get out of its way. It's meant to be shown this way. You may not understand it yet. But trust it, trust the unknown, trust all that comes out of you. Remember: you have everything you need."

I am letting myself go. I will get out of my head and I will allow myself to dance on paper. As if no one, not even myself, is watching. Break free from safety. Dance. Be weird, abstract. "Do I feel I like it or not?" I am trusting the process. The perfection of the natural process; teaching me everything on how to fulfil my potential. I will forget about the outcome and I will see, be and love the process. That's all that matters.

Creating is easy. The 'doing' it is easy. It's all about expressing the way you feel. Self-expressing. And if you understand that, then you also get that there is no good or bad. It's like breathing. You have to breathe. You just do it. At times I feel lonely in the process though. Longing for someone to tell me, "I like it." But I manage to get through it; to self-validate. This is probably part of the de-pleasing process: I am learning how to be fully content and satisfied with myself.

I love the playful tapping into my writing flow. I'm not taking it too seriously and I love it. No counting hours or words, just writing. I want to protect it, against everyone and everything that tries to pull me away from it. Not too fiercely though. I just want to be conscious of the things that might interrupt or negatively affect this sacred flow. Yesterday, I found myself at the intersection of this decision: go for a walk or stay inside and continue writing? I didn't take (what I thought was) the risk: I didn't move, I waved away the choice-point and continued tapping into my writing flow. It was divine. Because, as soon as I finished, it was sunset and I was ready to go for a walk. It was all perfect timing. I just love it when life shows you abundance: "You can have both, darling!" How life wants to help you. And if you let happen what needs to happen, then life can truly surprise you with its abundance.

It feels like I'm standing on a thin layer of ice. And that layer is becoming thinner and thinner. One day it might crack. At the same time, I have deep faith in myself. Life has shown me multiple times that the most important thing I can do, is to trust myself. To stop blaming myself, people or memories. It's good to have those memories come through me. But I can let them go now. They are not me.

Not anymore. The story of me, now, is so different. I am different. Do I know myself? Do I really see myself for who I am? Do I see not only the bad things but also what I'm good at? Am I brave enough to decide what is good for me now? Am I? Or will I be frightened by fear and let my light be dimmed? I can choose to shine bright, to set myself free. Writing my book is such a good and powerful act of being me. I feel that and I am ready to trust, deeply trust, the workings of me. Trust that by letting go, beautiful things can come my way. After all, it is in the act of surrender where imagination shows up.

"You are doing it. You are living life on your terms." His words moved me deeply and I could feel my inner strength. It makes me cry, even now. I feel so proud of my daily life. Even though some days are dark and some are light. I feel so proud of honouring my unique rhythm, of adhering to the flows inside, of being able to create, day after day. It makes me feel so fulfilled. So in touch with life.

It gives me so much meaning and value. If I look back to how life was just before I started writing the book, I can see that I have transformed so much, so quickly. I can hardly recognise the person I was before writing the book. She seems like an outdated version of me; one that no longer exists. It feels like this growth is continuing. It's still a bumpy ride, with hardly any predictions I can make about how it will all turn out. But I feel confident about my day-to-day practices. I know that, each day, I'm going to be here to create and write. To witness life unfolding itself exactly the way it's meant to.

A soft breeze reaches my skin. It's nothing, yet it is everything. It's the essence of life. This beauty, this form of life, streams through everything with such speed. Life moves so quickly that I can't wrap my head, or my body, around it. I keep on having these realisations: about time, about another day being over, about how quickly time travels. But at the same time, how slowly time goes... Oh, this contradiction! I've been feeling a similar whirlwind of emotions. Constantly moving from low to high, confusion to clarity, shock to calm. I've been noticing, especially last week, that I need more peace. Solitude. So I can deliberately and intentionally focus on what feels good for me. So I can create what I want to create without being distracted. It's intense: life is so powerful now. I have been feeling these weird sensations in my body, like butterflies or a free fall. Today I remembered: I should try believing more in positive outcomes than in negative outcomes. In abundance and not in lack. In infinite rather than finite possibilities.

At times it frightens me. Am I wasting my time? Falling behind on life, on where I should be by now? It creates adrenaline in my body. But do I want to change my life? No. Just the thought of trying to steer my life in a way so that it fits into predetermined boxes makes me freeze. I can't and I don't want to. At least, not at this point in my life. I want to continue going with the flow, explore new lands and build new worlds. Follow my instincts, my visions and bring my dreams into this world. That is me. I need to be free. But it's daunting at times, even though it is what I want. It's strange: the more Me I am, the more isolated I feel. I mean, who is really with me in this? Those who not only understand it, but who also are a living embodiment of it? I do experience judgment every now and then. People saying that I don't have it all together because I don't have X-Y-Z by my age. These projections leave one feeling like life is a ladder you have to climb. And only when you've climbed to a certain height, you may feel accomplished and worthy. If I take that in, it hurts. But when I let it go then, oh, I am free. Exactly where I need to be.

I feel unable to look back at my past and appreciate it. Something in me just refuses to look at my path and is much happier focusing on the path ahead of me. It's not pleasant, this feeling of not being able to appreciate the path you've walked on. Waving it all away with an "I wasn't at my best" or focusing on the mistakes that I've made. "Let's just move on" the mind commands. The thing is: I want to be able to look back and forgive myself. Be grateful for all that I've done, for everywhere I've been. Now, when I look at my past I can't help but see a mess. It truly feels like this messy pile that I have to work through. Like an old house that I've decided to renovate. I have to renovate my (perception of the) past; leave it in better conditions than it is now. I know it is time to clear myself and my past. I want to free myself of negativity. Become lighter and lighten the load within myself.

I need a ritual. Because it's not the easiest of tasks what I'm doing: going through my emotions and memories here on paper. Sifting them, sorting them, dissecting them, looking at them, describing them and facing them. I can't just dive into it. Well, I can. But it helps to set the stage; to slowly and respectfully go into this zone. I am going to burn some incense and candles. It calms me, this ritual of consciously preparing the space. It communicates to me: 'I am going to sit down and do this. I am going to be nice to myself and respect myself instead of rushing into the task.' I light the incense and the candles and automatically say: "Love. Please fill this room, my body and my mind, with love." Like magic, the room, my body and my mind fill up with warmth and love. The task at hand seems so much easier.

I love to be together. But I have to be aware that I'm not loving the being together more than the being alone. Although, as we know: I excel at being alone. I just have to make sure that I keep them in balance. That one stops and the other starts at the right time. Both are beautiful and good in their own way. The most important thing I seek for and validate in the people I surround myself with, is exactly that. Plus, it would be great if they, too, see and create or hold space for my potential. If they could help me be free of my conditioning. Oh, I love people who hold potential-parking-lots: a place where you can be whoever you desire to be, even though you're still buried beneath layers of conditioning. I like to think I hold those parking lots for others. In fact, I feel it's my main task in relation to others: to hold a place where they can come to and be themselves.

Note to self. As a self-loving human being, I focus on what I love doing in life. I don't need someone else's approval or validation besides my own. Important: I can give this to myself. The more I am learning to love myself and be kind to myself, the more I become aware of how well the other muscle is trained; how easy it is for me to frighten myself. To disempower myself or correct myself, just by thinking certain types of thoughts. Why would I allow that shrink-and-contract programming to be in there? The hopeful thing is: it is very easy to shift thoughts. I relax intensely when I think good thoughts. Still, it's new terrain for me. Somehow, it's daunting, this big silence. The body feels like: "Huh, what's this now?" I'm also getting used to how strong the heart feels now that it's getting more attention. It makes me emotional, like a breaking down of internal walls. A melting process.

The power of self-support. Oh, what self-support and self-encouragement can do to you. I mean, it's golden! It lifts me up to such a high level of being and of existing. It makes me feel strong, untouchable. Imagine if I could continue to guide myself like that.

When bad memories come up. I tell myself to restore the balance and bring up good memories. Because it is true: for every bamory (bad memory) there is a gemory (good memory). It's like trading cards: when life hands me a bamory card, I'll trade it with a gemory card. It helps me to get to a higher place where I can't judge — because, after all, these are all memories. No, I don't want to be held in a space where I feel I am holding grudges. I really don't like that place; it costs too much energy. For example, when I think about painful things people once said to me, I try to remember the good things they've done for me. And then, somehow, I get to a place of understanding that most people act from their own version of reality, from the level of consciousness they live in. (Of course, always interesting to observe where and why I got triggered. What are they inviting me to heal?) It is here where no one holds any power over me, nor influences the way I feel. I have free will. I live my life. I set my own vibration. I decide. And that feels very liberating, powerful, healing.

Today I have been taking myself through a self-love wash. During my walks in the forest, in the shower, whilst cooking: I have been talking to myself in the most affirmative and loving ways. Especially when my mind started making some noise. I experienced a shift last night, when lots of old thoughts started popping up. I acknowledged them and waved them away by saying: "Oh mind, I love how creative you are, you are so good at telling stories. From now on, let's tell the right ones." The moment I said that, I empowered myself. My system relaunched. I now feel like sharing with you some of my own affirmations, thereby taking you with me on a quick ride through my self-love wash: "I am where I need to be. I am who I am meant to be. I know all I need to know. I possess a deep inner knowledge which I am willing to share with everyone who invites me. The more energy I invest towards rebalancing myself, the more I can be of service to others and the world. Everything I create, I share with the world as an offer of love. I work with energy instead of against it. I love me. I love me."

I never ever doubt if writing this book is the right choice. From the moment I chose to start writing this book, I dove straight into my life's purpose. And now it feels so normal to be me like this. I feel that I'm home, that this is me. It feels so liberating. Such a heavy weight has been lifted off my shoulders and chest because of this book. Life makes so much more sense to me know. This book has been a deep journey into myself. The more I accept that I'm different (me), that I'm meant to live an unconventional life, the easier life feels.

I'm meant to be blessing the world. Blessing it with joy, beauty, the delicious life energy that flows through me and the way I transform it into creativity.
Whenever I'm creating, I can sense myself balancing between self-awareness and self-awkwardness. I often ask myself: "Am I weird?" Self-awareness is neutral. Self-awkwardness, now that's a conditioned part. That's the Me bumping into the experiences it's had while being alive and in contact with humans. But there can't be awkwardness in the now. It's just me expressing life as it's running through me and as I'm experiencing it. It's just me being me. Now I might think it's awkward, people might think it's awkward, but the force that is helping me to do this, this life joy, most certainly doesn't think it's awkward.

I am laughing at my friends the creations. I enjoy their company in a wondrous way. I enjoy the wonder of us as human beings being able to create something that has never existed before. It's magic, to create your own world, to put down your visions. So highly empowering, too. When I'm illustrating, my mind goes into deep reflective mode. Thoughts are floating by; it's a meditative state. I receive new insights and awarenesses. It's healthy for me. Creating is healthy for me. To create using my pain, to describe how something feels, to play with it, turn it inside out, upside down. It's such a powerful awareness to understand that you yourself have the power to transform yourself and all that you feel. To not feel helpless but to know that: when I feel this way, I can use it in my creative process. Pain, as well as chaos and confusion, are all gifts to transmute into art. —

pouring out my heart in gratitude

Huub Habets — You are the living embodiment of unconditional support. Thank you for loving me so deeply and for believing in me. Thank you for giving me space and support to realise my dreams and thereby go through a deep inner transformation.

Beagle Elly — Thank you for your love, companionship, big velvety listening ears and for the cuddling when I need(ed) it the most. You truly know what this book means to me. I love you.

Frank Geraerts — You've witnessed (and perhaps even ignited) my radical change. Thank you for seeing the real me, my gifts and my potential so early on in my life. Thank you for believing in me, for pushing my buttons, for your consistent support and your patience.

Bruce Mau — Oh, how I enjoy(ed) our one-on-one talks. I listened with fascination to you sharing wisdom and anecdotes and to your passionate laughter. Most of all, thank you for allowing me to look through your eyes at my book.

Maarten Schrevel — We share a deep passion for the same country and language. Throughout the years, you've taught me so much. It was our correspondence that made me fall in love, again, with writing. I am forever grateful to you for that.

Carry Somers — My life changed when you invited me to stay at your home in England. It was then and there that I knew: I want to live here. And so I made the change. Thank you for guiding me home.

Sacred Sites and Architecture — Ben, Margaret, Julia, Coco, Eco, Romke, Jitske, Yanik, Bruce and Kearie: our weekly gatherings have meant, and still mean, a lot to me. Thank you all for sharing your genius, your big hearts and your endless dedication to designing, improving and protecting our world(s).

Paps and mams — How can I ever thank you for providing me with a safe home during the most challenging time of my life? Thank you for being there for me, for supporting me, for listening to me and for allowing me to be me.

about the author

Elise Crutzen (Maastricht, 1991) is an artist based in the United Kingdom and the
Netherlands. She holds an MA in Comunicación de Moda y Belleza VOGUE and
a BSc in European Studies (Communication Management). She works as a writer
and communications consultant. Besides writing poetry and prose, Elise expresses
herself through photography and earth paintings; collecting, processing and
applying earth pigments from over the world on recycled denim canvas. As for this
book, one could say it has been a lifetime in the making. **www.elisecrutzen.com**

this is tree-less paper, made from agricultural waste

Oh... I couldn't. I couldn't write a book, proclaiming my love for nature, and then print it on paper made from trees. My heart hurt when imagining it. I understood the change started with me. I had to vocalise my truth and wonder, trust and believe a different way existed. I sought solutions and people. And I found them! Oh, how happy I felt when I found out that I could print these words on **PaperWise.**

each book:

 contains **± 0,54 kg** PaperWise paper

 prevents **± 0,01 tree** from being cut

 prevents **± 0,70 kg** CO2-equivalent ≈ to **6 km** car driving

 gives **± 0,46 kg** agricultural waste a second life on annual basis

This book has been printed on PaperWise. A new generation of paper and board with a very low environmental impact and a significant social contribution, made from agricultural waste. PaperWise gives the stems and leaves that remain after harvesting our food crops a second life by processing it into high-quality paper and board. www.paperwise.eu

Published in December 2022 by Elise Crutzen in Margraten (NL)
Written in Bagshot Park and Windsor Forest (UK)
Printed by Drukkerij Walters in Maastricht (NL)

Illustrations, photography and design by Elise Crutzen

Photography locations:
Bath, Brecon Beacons, Dartmoor National Park, Jurassic Coast,
Llyn y Fan Fach, Snowdonia National Park, South Hayling, Surrey Hills,
Swinley Forest, Tenby, Windsor Forest, Windsor Great Park (UK)

People who've helped bring this book to life:
Benedict, Bruce, Frank, Huub, Lilian, Maarten,
Marieke, Michel, Miranda, Sabine, Pascal

The contents of this book may be shared, please mention:
Elise Crutzen/ @elisecrutzen
Use #onmywayhome to share your journey

ISBN 978 9 09036 659 3

if you love this book
pass it on to someone
you know will love it too
so that this book, too,
may find its way home